HISTORY & GEOGRA
A WORLD OF NEIGHB

MW00965035

CONTENTS

Author: **Ruth Guthrie, M.A.**
Editor: Richard W. Wheeler, M.A.Ed.
Consulting Editor: Howard Stitt, Th.M., Ed.D.
Revision Editor: Alan Christopherson, M.S.

Alpha Omega Publications®

804 N. 2nd Ave. E., Rock Rapids, IA 51246-1759

Learn with our friends:

When you see me, I will help your teacher explain the exciting things you are expected to do.

When you do actions with me, you will learn how to write, draw, match words, read, and much more.

You and I will learn about matching words, listening, drawing, and other fun things in your lessons.

Follow me and I will show you new, exciting truths, that will help you learn and understand what you study. Let's learn!

A WORLD OF NEIGHBORHOODS

Many, many people live in the world.
Each one is different from all the others.
Yet people in every land have many
things that are the same. You will read
about things that all families need.
You will read about some different things
people do in different countries. As you
read, remember that the same God who
loves you loves all people.

Read these objectives. They will tell what you will be able
to do when you have finished this LIFEPAC®.

1. You will be able to list at least four things families
   everywhere need.
2. You will be able to tell some of the things that are
   the same about communities in any land.
3. You will be able to tell what a custom is.
4. You will be able to name some Thanksgiving customs.
5. You will be able to name some Easter customs.
6. You will be able to give some examples of New Year's
   customs.
7. You will be able to identify different Christmas
   customs.

NEW WORDS

angel (an gel). A messenger from God.

bread. A food made from flour.

camel (ca mel). An animal that is used on the desert for work because it can go a long time without water.

change. To become different.

clothes. The coverings for the body.

community (com mu ni ty). All the people living in the same place.

custom (cus tom). A habit learned by a community or group of people.

envelope (en ve lope). A paper cover inside which a letter is put.

flour. Ground up grain used to make bread.

goods. Things for sale.

grain. The seed from wheat, corn, and other cereal grasses.

habit (ha bit). Something you are used to doing.

harvest (har vest). Gathering in the grain and other foods.

income (in come). The money that is earned.

law. Rules made for the people to live by.

lily (lil y). A plant with tall stems and bell-shaped flowers.

piñata (pi ña ta). A paper animal filled with candy for children.

rice. A grain.

services (serv ic es). Helping others.

share. To let others do something.

shelter (shel ter). Something that protects from weather or
    danger.

special (spe cial). Different from anything else.

stocking (stock ing). A covering for the leg.

straw. The stem left after grain is cut.

trailer (trail er). A house on wheels.

wheat. A grain.

These words will appear in **boldface** (darker print) the first time they are used.

I. WORLDWIDE FAMILY NEEDS

People live in families all over the world. In some ways your family might be very different from your friend's family. But you still have many things that are the same. Families work and play together. They love and care for each other. You will read about some things families need to live. Think about your own family as you read.

WORDS TO STUDY	
bread	A food made from flour.
clothes	The coverings for the body.

flour		Ground up grain used to make bread.
grain		The seed from wheat, corn, and other cereal grasses.
rice		A grain.
shelter	(shel ter)	Something that protects from weather or danger.
special	(spe cial)	Different from anything else.
trailer	(trail er)	A house on wheels.
wheat		A grain.

Ask your teacher to say these words with you.

Teacher Check _____

Initial   Date

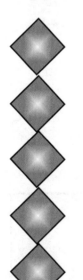
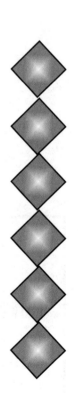

FAMILIES IN THE WORLD NEED FOOD

All the people in the world need food to live. Different foods are eaten in different countries. Each country has some foods that are **special** to that country.

Rice is the main food for many people. Rice is grown in fields of water. It is eaten alone or with other foods.

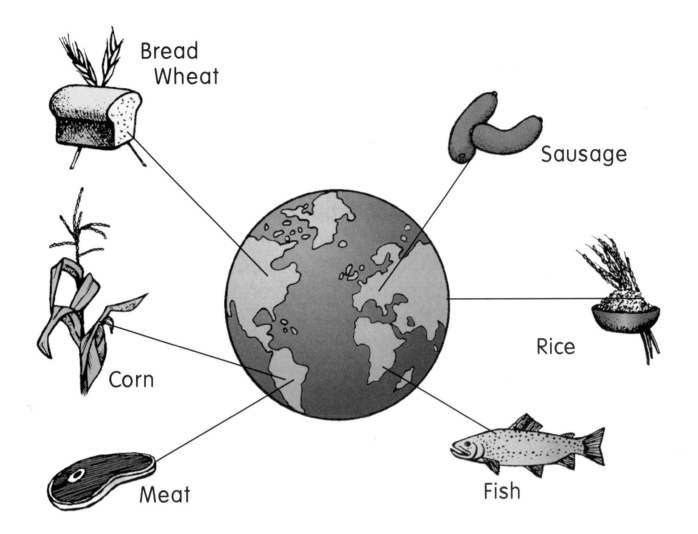

Bread
Wheat

Sausage

Rice

Corn

Meat

Fish

Corn and **wheat** are **grains** that many people eat. The seeds of corn and wheat are made into **flour**. Flour is made into many kinds of food. You eat **bread** made from flour. People in other lands eat other foods made from flour.

In some countries people do not have enough to eat. In other lands people can choose what they want to eat. You live in a land that has a lot of food.

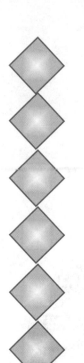
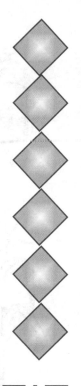

If your mother asks, "What would you like to eat for dinner today?" you should be very thankful. Many children do not have enough to eat. They are glad for any food at all.

What some people eat may seem strange to you. What you eat may seem strange to someone else. Food from one place to another may be different. One thing is the same. People in all lands need food.

Look at the picture. Print your answer.

1.1   How are these boys the same?

_____

_____

Name three (3) important things that people eat.

1.2 _____

1.3 _____

1.4 _____

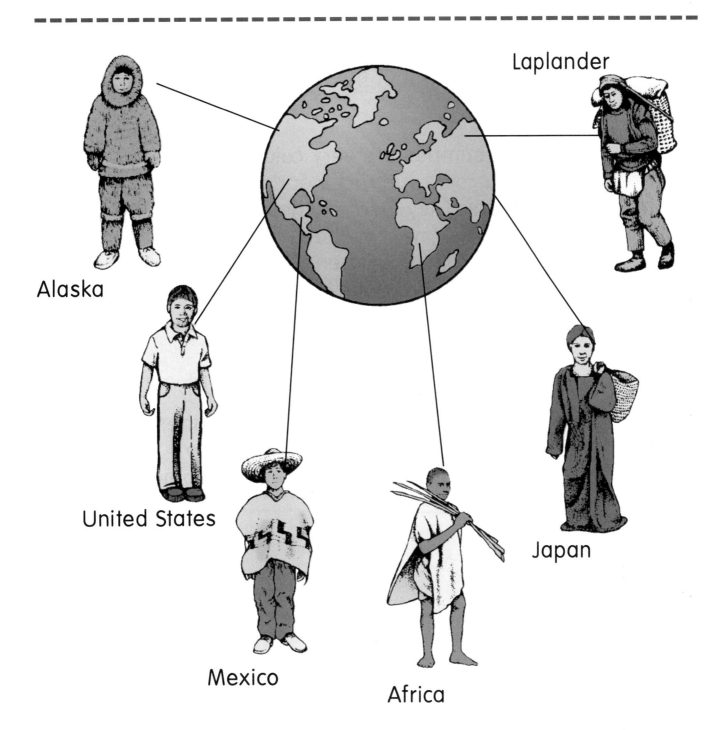

Laplander

Alaska

United States

Mexico

Africa

Japan

FAMILIES IN THE WORLD NEED CLOTHES

Some countries are hot. Other countries are cold. In the hot countries people wear **clothes** that are just right for that land. The clothes keep the sun from the people. The people do not get too hot.

People in other hot countries wear few clothes. They do not get too hot under the trees.

Some countries are very cold. The people in cold countries wear clothes to keep warm. They wear clothes that keep warm air next to them. Mothers might say to their children, "Remember to put on your coat!" or "I don't want you to catch cold. Please wear your cap and mittens."

People in other countries may have clothes that look funny to you. But your clothes might look funny to them! Clothes might be different, but one thing is the same. All people in the world need clothes.

 **Write** HOT **or** COLD **under the kind of weather each child lives in.**

1.5 _____ _____ _____ _____

 Do these reading activities.

1.6 All of the words in the list end with ck. Some of the ck words sound like trick. Write those words under trick. Then write the other words under track.

pick	lack	stick	stack
brick	tack	sack	tick
pack	rack	lick	slick

trick   **track**

_____   _____

_____   _____

_____   _____

_____   _____

_____   _____

_____   _____

1.7 The letters tch are in each of the words you need in these sentences. The first letter is given to you. Add a vowel and tch to each beginning letter to make a word that makes sense in each sentence.

a. The boy ran to c _____ the ball.

b. He looked at his w _____ to see what time it was.

c. Mr. Turner picked up a m _____ to light the fire.

d. Mother made a b _____ of cookies.

• •

FAMILIES IN THE WORLD NEED SHELTER

People live in many places on the earth. In every place that people live, they need a **shelter**. A shelter keeps people warm where it is cold. A shelter keeps the sun off the people where it is hot. A shelter keeps people dry when it rains.

People's homes are their shelters. Homes are made of many different things. Some homes are made of stones. Some homes are made of wood. Some homes are made of grass. Other homes are tents or **trailers**. Some people live on houseboats.

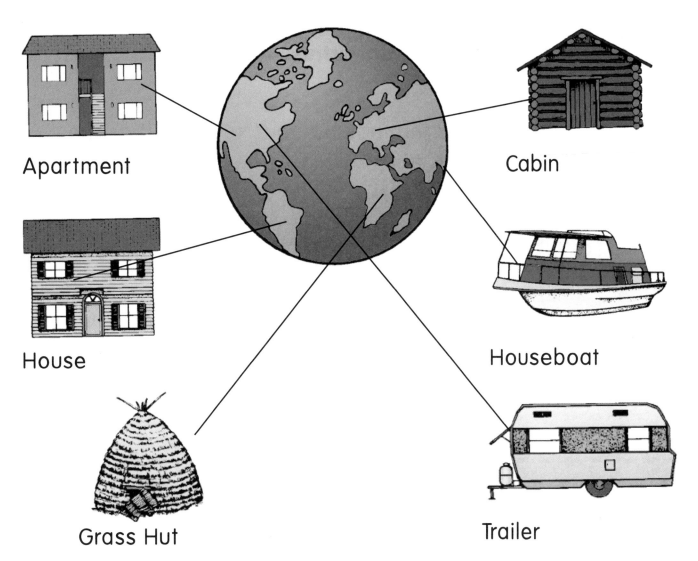

Apartment

Cabin

House

Houseboat

Grass Hut

Trailer

Many different kinds of homes are in the world. But one thing is the same. All people in the world need to live in a shelter.

Draw a line to match the words.

1.8	tents and trailers	the homes of people in all the world
1.9	stone homes	walls keep out the sun's heat
1.10	houseboats	easy to move around
1.11	shelter	not enough room on the land

Do these reading activities.

1.12   Circle the word that has the /ou/ sound in it as the ou sound in house.

about   would   country   ground
could   fourth   mouth   round
found   young   bounce   brought
should   trouble   soup   shout

1.13   Some words end with the letters nt as in went. Circle each word that ends in nt like went.

tent   cone   plant   tree
point   man   apple   paint

- -

FAMILIES IN THE WORLD NEED LOVE

Every family needs love. Children need to know that their mother and father love them. Children need to love their mother and their father. A mother and a father need to love each other.

The mother and the father should teach the children. Children learn from their mother and father. Children should do what mother and father say.

All families in the world need God's love. People can know God's love through His Son, Jesus.

Name two (2) jobs you do at home.

1.14 _____

1.15 _____

Name two things your mother or father teach you.

1.16 _____

1.17 _____

Cross out the sentences that are not true.

1.18 Children know everything there is to know.

1.19 Children learn things from their mother and father.

1.20 Every family needs love.

1.21 The mother and father should not teach the children.

Teacher Check _____

Initial   Date

For this Self Test, study what you have read and done. The Self Test will check what you remember.

SELF TEST 1

Match the sentences with the right picture.

1.01   A good shelter in a
        hot land.

1.02   A good shelter in a
        cold land.

1.03   A shelter that can be moved
        from place to place.

Circle the right answer for each sentence.

1.04   Homes are different where it is hot and where it is
        cold.

                    yes   no

1.05   Everyone eats the same thing in all the world.
                    yes   no

1.06   Most people wear clothes to keep them warm where it is cold.

yes   no

1.07   The mother and father should teach the children.

yes   no

Check (✔) the sentences that are true. Put O if the sentence is not true.

1.08   _____   Rice is the main food for many people.

1.09   _____   People everywhere need a shelter to live in.

1.010   _____   All families everywhere need God's love.

1.011   _____   All people wear the same kind of clothes.

Name four things that families need.

1.012   _____

1.013   _____

1.014   _____

1.015   _____

EACH ANSWER, 1 POINT

12
15

Teacher Check _____

Initial   Date

My Score

page 15 (fifteen)

II. WORLDWIDE NEIGHBORHOODS

You have learned that a **community** is all the people who live in one place under the same **laws**. This part of your LIFEPAC will help you remember some of the things you have learned about communities. You will read about some of the ways communities all over the world are alike. You will also read about a few of the ways communities are different. Think about your own community as you read. Thinking about your own community will help you remember what you read.

WORDS TO STUDY

change		To become different.
community	(com mu ni ty)	All the people living in the same place.
goods		Things for sale.
income	(in come)	The money that is earned.
law		Rules made for the people to live by.
services	(serv ic es)	Helping others.
share		To let others do something.

Ask your teacher to say these words with you.

Teacher Check _____

Initial   Date

COMMUNITIES SHARE

You and your neighbors are part of the same community. You live by the same laws. You use the same parks and stores. People in your community go to the same doctors. The same firefighters and police officers help you and your neighbors.

Seamstress

Farmer

House builder

People in communities do different kinds of work. Some people in a community work with **goods**. Farmers grow food. Some people make clothes. Other people build houses. Many people in a community work with **services**. Some people are teachers and work at schools. Others fix cars and work in garages. Some people work in banks.

Others work in churches. People need each other. People **share**. They live in communities so they can help each other.

Draw a line through the sentences that are not true.

2.1   Communities are the same in every way.
2.2   Communities share goods and services.
2.3   People in communities do not need things.
2.4   Communities have many different workers.

Do these reading activities.

2.5   The /er/ sound as in worker is in many words. The letters er, ir, or ur often have the same sound.

Print the words under the letters that are in the words.

flower	surprise	dirt	first
hurry	after	her	third
church			

er	ir	ur
_____	_____	_____
_____	_____	_____
_____	_____	_____

2.6 Write the missing letters (er, ur, ir). Draw a line to match the words that are the same.

a. curl   s_____ _____vice
b. service   c_____ _____l
c. bird   b_____ _____d
d. girl   oth_____ _____
e. other   n_____ _____se
f. nurse   g_____ _____l

COMMUNITIES NEED INCOME

The workers in a community earn an **income**. Income is the money people get for doing work. People can spend their income on the things they need and want. Some communities have many workers. Many people do many jobs in the community. Other communities have fewer jobs, so fewer people live there. If a community is big or if it is small, it has people in it who help each other and earn an income.

Fill in the dot in front of the word that goes in the blank.

2.7 Money earned for work is _____ .

     ○ outcome   ○ income

2.8 Selling bread is a way of giving _____ .

     ○ goods   ○ services

2.9 Fixing cars is giving _____ .

     ○ goods   ○ services

2.10 Big cities have _____ jobs.

     ○ many   ○ few

● ●

COMMUNITIES CHANGE

Long ago people came to different places to live. Towns grew where people wanted to stay and work. People built houses, stores, and churches. The towns grew into cities. Parts of farms were covered with houses and city buildings. Trees were cut down to make room for growing cities. Soon, some of the old buildings were too small. Other buildings were not used. These buildings were knocked down so new ones could be built.

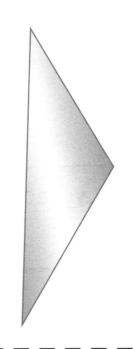

Some people move to a city and stay there. Their children grow up. They might stay, or they might move. Other people stay and work for a short time. Then they move to another town. If a town has no more jobs, everyone moves away. Only the buildings are left. After many years, even the buildings might be gone. Communities in the world are **changing** all the time.

- - - - - - - - - - - - - - - - - - - -

 Draw a line from the word to the meaning.

2.11	changing	many people and buildings in one place
2.12	community	a group of people who live by the same laws
2.13	income	money you get for doing work
2.14	worker	not staying the same
2.15	city	goods and services
		someone who works

 Teacher Check _____
Initial   Date

Think about your community.

2.16   Write about your community. Use good sentences. Be sure part of your writing tells how your community shares. Also, tell about the kind of jobs the people in your community have. Tell about how your community is changing. Use other paper.

 Teacher Check _____
Initial   Date

 Study what you have read and done for this Self Test. This Self Test will check what you remember of this part and other parts you have read.

SELF TEST 2

Circle yes **or** no.

2.01   All families are alike in some ways.
                        yes   no
2.02   All families are different in some ways.
                        yes   no

Put S by the things that are the same about families. Put D by the things that are different about families.

2.03   need for love   _____
2.04   need for clothes   _____
2.05   kind of clothes   _____
2.06   need for food   _____
2.07   kind of food   _____

HISTORY & GEOGRAPHY

2 0 5

LIFEPAC TEST

21/26

Name _____

Date _____

Score _____

HISTORY AND GEOGRAPHY 205: LIFEPAC TEST

EACH ANSWER, 1 POINT

Put a check (✔) by the words that make true sentences.

1. Families in every land

    _____ need food.   _____ need clothes.

    _____ live in tents.   _____ need shelter.

    _____ need love.   _____ have gardens.

2. Communities in every land

    _____ have different customs.

    _____ share many goods and services.

    _____ have big schools.

    _____ have many different workers.

    _____ are changing.

    _____ have workers earning income.

3. People in every community

    _____ learn from each other.

    _____ have special customs.

    _____ need God's love.

    _____ need the same customs.

4. Some Thanksgiving customs are

    _____ eating Pilgrims.

    _____ giving thanks to God.

    _____ eating special foods.

    _____ taking food to churches.

5.   Some New Year's customs are

_____ horns and lists.

_____ skipping around a fire.

_____ climbing a mountain.

Match the country with the custom.

6.	"first footing"	England
7.	Harvest Festival Day	Scotland
8.	money in red envelopes	Mexico
9.	piñatas	China

Match the custom with the holiday.

10.	tree lights	Easter
11.	painting eggs	Christmas
12.	feeling pigs	Thanksgiving
13.	eating together	New Year's

Answer the question using good sentences.

14.   What is a custom? _____

_____

_____

NOTES

2.08	number of children	_____
2.09	need for shelter	_____
2.010	kind of shelter	_____

Circle yes **or** no.

2.011   All communities are alike in some ways.

                    yes   no

2.012   All communities are different in some ways.

                    yes   no

**Put S by the things that are the same about communities.
Put D by the things that are different about communities.**

2.013	_____	People share goods and services.
2.014	_____	People need each other.
2.015	_____	number of people in the community
2.016	_____	Workers earn income.
2.017	_____	how close neighbors live to each other
2.018	_____	the work people do

EACH ANSWER, 1 POINT

$\dfrac{14}{18}$

Teacher Check _____

                        Initial   Date

My Score

III. WORLDWIDE CUSTOMS

You have learned many things from your family. Most children learn how to act from their family. You have heard your mother or father say, "Did you say please and thank you?" or "Don't talk with food in your mouth!" When you learn these things, you know how to act. When you do something over and over, it becomes a **habit**. A habit is something that is learned. When a group of people learn the same habit, it is a **custom**. A custom is a habit learned by a group of people. Some customs come from the Bible. Other customs are made up by people.

Families in different parts of the world do things in different ways. They have different customs. A custom is something people do over and over. Fathers and mothers teach their children customs. Children grow up and teach their children the same customs. Years and years go by. People still have the same customs. They are passed from family to family. Customs that seem strange to you are not strange to others. People have different ways of doing things. You will learn about some of these different customs in this part of your LIFEPAC.

WORDS TO STUDY

angel	(an gel)	A messenger from God.
camel	(cam el)	An animal that is used on the desert for work because it can go a long time without water.
custom	(cus tom)	A habit learned by a community or group of people.
envelope	(en ve lope)	A paper cover inside which a letter is put.
habit	(hab it)	Something you are used to doing.
harvest	(har vest)	Gathering in the grain and other foods.
lily	(lil y)	A plant with tall stems and bell shaped flowers.
piñata	(pi ña ta)	A paper animal filled with candy for children.
stocking	(stock ing)	A covering for the leg.
straw		The stem left after grain is cut.

SPECIAL WORDS

America	England	
Austria	February	
Belgium	Indian	Norway
Bethlehem	January	November
Canada	Japan	Pilgrims
Christ Child	Joseph	Poland

Russia	Thanksgiving Day	Vienna
Scotland	United States	Wise Men
Sunday		

Ask your teacher to say these words with you.

Teacher Check _____

Initial   Date

THANKSGIVING

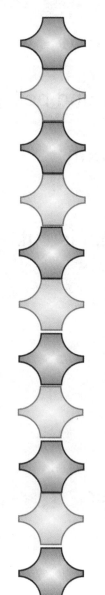

People in many different countries have a special day to thank God for all things. A long time ago, people called Pilgrims came to America. They had many hard times. They worked hard. The Indians helped them grow food. The Indians helped the Pilgrims learn how to live in the new land. The Pilgrims **harvested** the food. They were thankful. They thanked God for helping them. They asked the Indians to come to a big dinner. They ate the food that they had found in the new land.

People in England give thanks on Harvest Festival Day. They bring food to the churches. The food is then taken by the children and shared with the poor people of the community.

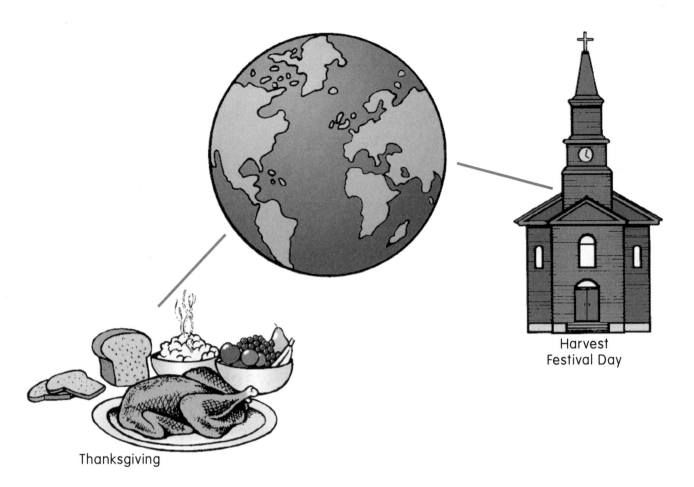

Thanksgiving

Harvest
Festival Day

Canada has a day of Thanksgiving,
too. These days are in the fall when
food is harvested.

People in the United States have Thanksgiving
Day in November. Most people eat
special foods for Thanksgiving dinner. It
is the **custom**.

Check the right answer.

3.1   Thanksgiving Day is a good name for this custom
because

_____ the people eat much food.
_____ the pilgrims had Indian friends.
_____ the people were giving thanks to God.

page 27 (twenty-seven)

Circle the month in which you have Thanksgiving Day.

3.2   March   November   July

EASTER

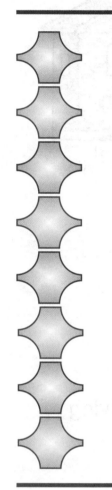

Every year people remember when Jesus came back to life. Easter is the name of this special day. Jesus came back to life on the first day of the week. Many Christians have the custom of going to church on the first day of the week. The first day of the week is Sunday.

Year after year people remember this wonderful day. It is a custom in many churches to meet early on Easter morning. In these sunrise services, the people remember that Jesus came back to life.

Read Mark 16:1 through 8. The story of Jesus coming back to life is in these verses. Read the story to a friend.

Friend's name _____

People bring **lilies** to church
on Easter Sunday in the United States.
Some people believe that the lily means
something good and beautiful. Others
think of the lily as something in the
ground. Then up come the green leaves!
Out come the beautiful white flowers!
Lilies help people to think of Jesus being
in the ground and coming back to life.
Bringing lilies to church on Easter is a
custom.

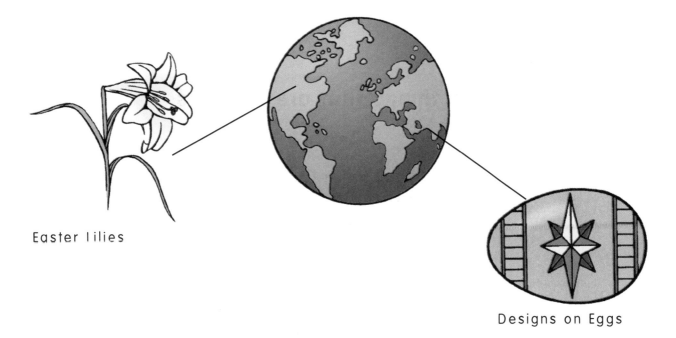

Easter lilies

Designs on Eggs

Another Easter custom is to have
special eggs at Easter time. New life
comes from eggs. The eggs remind people
that new life comes from Jesus. People in
Russia and Poland put beautiful pictures
on eggs. In other countries people make
the eggs different colors.

Check two (2) answers for each sentence.

3.3 The story of the first Easter

_____ is about eggs and lilies.
_____ is told in the Bible.
_____ is about Jesus coming back to life.

3.4 Easter

_____ is always on a Sunday.
_____ helps us remember that Jesus is alive.
_____ is the same as Christmas.

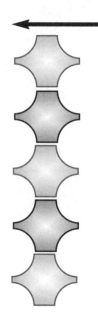

Check the things that are customs.

3.5 _____ eating with chopsticks
_____ eating with forks
_____ snow and rain

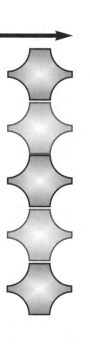

THE NEW YEAR

New Year's Eve is the last day of the year. We have a custom that people stay up late on New Year's Eve. They want to wait for the new year to start.

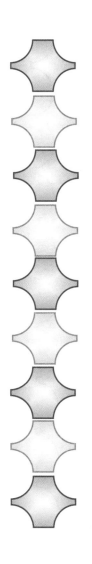

When the new year starts the people blow horns and say, "Happy New Year!" Many parades are in different cities on New Year's Day. Some people make lists of things they want to do in the new year. The good times, the parades, and the lists are customs.

In a little town in England people gather around a fire. A band plays songs. The people skip around the fire. The custom is for the people to stay until the fire goes out. They say "Happy New Year" in this way. The custom is so old that no one knows how it started.

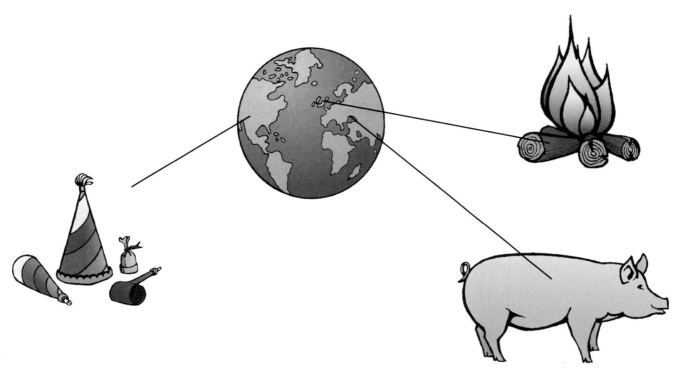

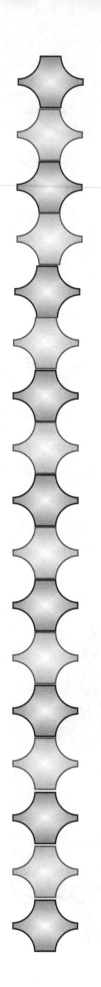

In Japan, people eat fish on New Year's Day. They hope the fish will make them strong.

Farmers in Belgium say "Happy New Year" to all their animals on New Year's morning.

People in Vienna, Austria chase a pig on New Year's morning. If they feel the pig, they believe they will have good luck.

Long ago in Scotland the people wanted to have good luck. The custom of having someone bring good luck on New Year's Eve was called "first footing." The first boy to come to a house on New Year's Eve brought good luck. If a girl was the first to come to a door, she brought bad luck. Only boys went out so that everyone would have good luck in the new year. First footing is still a custom in Scotland on New Year's Eve.

The Chinese New Year is not the first day in January. It is at the end of January or the first part of February. Chinese fathers and mothers put money in a little red **envelope**. They put the

envelope by their sleeping child. They put the money in a red envelope because red means good luck in China. People who believe the Bible believe in "God's blessing" rather than "good luck."

Read Romans 8:28 in your Bible and talk about this verse with a friend.

Friend's name _____

Check the right answers.

3.6 The last day of the year is

_____ the Chinese New Year.

_____ New Year's Eve.

_____ New Year's Day.

3.7 "First footing" is a custom in

_____ Japan.

_____ Austria.

_____ Scotland.

3.8 People in Vienna, Austria, think it is good luck

_____ to feel a pig on New Year's Day.

_____ to eat hot dogs for breakfast.

_____ to put money in red envelopes.

3.9   People who believe the Bible believe

_____   in good luck.

_____   in God's blessing.

_____   in "first footing."

Write two things that you would want to do in a new year.

3.10   _____

        _____

3.11   _____

        _____

CHRISTMAS

People in different countries have different ways of thinking about Christmas. They have different Christmas customs.

You think of Christmas when you see a tree with lights and colored balls on it. You give your friends and family things they would like to have. Christmas is a happy time. You go to church. You read the story of the baby Jesus. You have fun with your family and friends. You have customs that you think are special.

In England and in the United States, children hang up **stockings** on Christmas Eve. On the morning of Christmas Day they look in the stocking. It is filled with good things.

On Christmas Eve, the children in France put shoes by the door. The Christ Child is said to put good things in them.

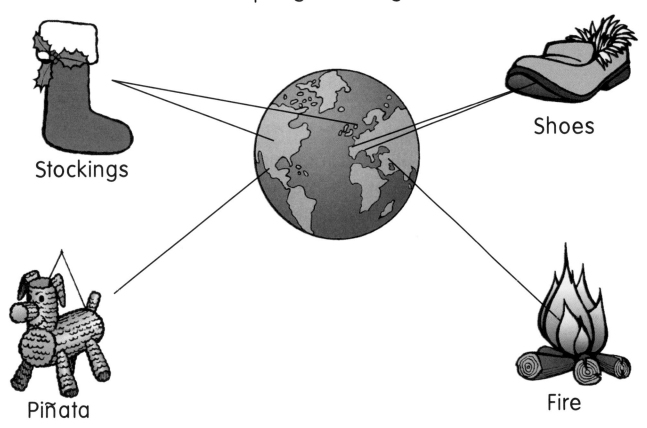

Stockings

Shoes

Piñata

Fire

Twelve days after Christmas the children in Spain put **straw** in their shoes. The straw is for the **camels** of the Wise Men. The camels are to pass by, eat the straw, and leave good things.

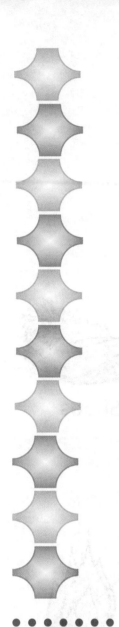

Children in Norway give food to the birds. They hang grain and fat on a tree outside the house. The birds have food to eat when the snow is on the ground.

Many people give gifts to each other at Christmas. The custom comes from the gifts the Wise Men brought to the young child, Jesus.

In Mexico many children have a piñata at Christmas time. A piñata is made of paper. Sometimes it looks like a little animal. The piñata is filled with candy and other good things. The piñata hangs by a rope. Children have their eyes covered. They try to hit the piñata with a big stick. When the piñata breaks, everyone runs to pick up the candy and other good things.

• •

Print in the right answers.

3.12   What are two (2) countries where children hang up their stockings?

_____   _____

3.13   What are two (2) countries where children put out their shoes?

_____   _____

On Christmas Eve many families in Norway stand around the Christmas tree. They hold hands and walk slowly around the tree. They sing Christmas songs as they walk. Walking around the tree is a Christmas custom.

In Syria on Christmas Eve, people may sit around a fire. They listen to a story with the family. When the fire goes out, everyone jumps over where the fire had been. Then each one makes a wish. The fire and story are Christmas customs.

If you were in Syria on Christmas Eve, what would you wish?

3.14

_____

_____

Draw a line from the country to the Christmas custom.

3.15

Spain	tree
Norway	straw in shoes
United States	story around a fire
Mexico	feed birds
Syria	piñata

Think about Christmas customs in other lands.

3.16   Read in a special book about Christmas customs.
Write about one Christmas custom you like. Use other
paper.

Teacher Check _____
                        Initial   Date

Countries have different Christmas
customs. The Christmas story is the
same in every country. Read about
the birth of Jesus in your Bible.

Find the story in Luke 2:1 through 20.

Teacher Check _____
                        Initial   Date

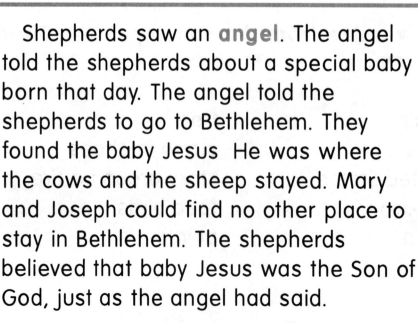

Shepherds saw an **angel**. The angel
told the shepherds about a special baby
born that day. The angel told the
shepherds to go to Bethlehem. They
found the baby Jesus He was where
the cows and the sheep stayed. Mary
and Joseph could find no other place to
stay in Bethlehem. The shepherds
believed that baby Jesus was the Son of
God, just as the angel had said.

The birthday of the Christ Child was thought to have been on different days for many years After awhile Christmas was put on December 25.

At Christmas you might see stockings, piñatas, trees, and toys. Different countries have different Christmas customs. The real meaning of Christmas is the birthday of Jesus. Jesus came into the world to save us from sin. Read John 3:16.

 Circle your answer to the question.

3.17   Mary and Joseph found no room in Bethlehem for Jesus. Have you made room in your life for Jesus?

    yes   I do not know

Christmas and Easter do not mean much until you know Jesus lived, was killed, and lives again for you. If you do not know if Jesus is in your heart, talk to your teacher about it.

Fill in the right words from the word bank.

3.18	At Christmas many girls and ___ ___ ___ ___
3.19	think of getting lots of ___ ___ ___ ___ .
3.20	Horns and bells make lots of ___ ___ ___ ___ ___
3.21	but they do not give lasting ___ ___ ___ ___ .
3.22	A child went shopping with some ___ ___ ___ ___ ___ .
3.23	His dime some other small ones ___ ___ ___ ___ ___ .
3.24	I heard him say in a loud , clear ___ ___ ___ ___ ___ .
3.25	"I'll give to Jesus. I've made my ___ ___ ___ ___ ."

WORD BANK

joins

noise

coins

joys

voice

boys

choice

toys

Write the answer to the question. Use good sentences.

3.26   What is a custom? _____

_____

_____

_____

_____

Fill in the blanks to finish the Christmas story.
You may use your Bible.

Read Luke 2:1 through 20.

Bethlehem	peace	Jesus	clothes	inn
God	joy	shepherds	angel	

3.27   Joseph and Mary went to _____ to be taxed.

3.28   There was no room for them in the _____ .

3.29   They stayed in a stable. _____ was born that night.

3.30   Mary put baby Jesus in swaddling _____ .

3.31   An _____ of the Lord told the

_____ ,

3.32   "Fear not, for I bring you good tidings of great

_____ ."

3.33   Many angels said "Glory to _____ in the highest, and

3.34   on earth, _____ , good will toward men."

Think about customs.

3.35   Write about some customs that you and your family have. Name at least four.

 Teacher Check _____

                         Initial   Date

Review

REVIEW Review   Study what you have read and done for this last Self Test. This Self Test will check what you remember in your studies of all parts in this LIFEPAC. The last Self Test will tell you what parts of the LIFEPAC you will need to study again.

SELF TEST 3

Think about customs. Mark each custom with the right letter. Write N if it goes with New Year's, E if it goes with Easter, T if it goes with Thanksgiving, C if it goes with Christmas.

3.01 _____ Jesus' birthday

3.02 _____ a Sunday in spring

3.03 _____ white lilies

3.04 _____ January 1

3.05 _____ "first footing"

3.06 _____ straw in shoes

3.07 _____ pictures on eggs

3.08 _____ angels talking to shepherds

3.09 _____ piñatas and stockings

3.010 _____ Pilgrims

3.011 _____ sunrise services

3.012 _____ Harvest Festival Day

Name four things that families need.

3.013 _____ 3.015 _____

3.014 _____ 3.016 _____

Write yes **or** no **on the line in front of each sentence.**

3.017 _____ People share goods and services.

3.018 _____ All people need to wear clothes.

3.019	_____	The number of people in a community is always the same.
3.020	_____	All homes are the same.
3.021	_____	Everyone has the same customs.
3.022	_____	Income is the money you earn for doing work.

Put a (✔) by the words that are true.

3.023   Communities in all lands.

_____   have no schools.

_____   are changing.

_____   have people earning income.

_____   have different customs.

3.024   Some Thanksgiving customs are

_____   thanking God.

_____   tree lights.

_____   eating a special dinner.

Answer the question in good sentences.

3.025   What is a custom? _____

_____

_____

EACH ANSWER, 1 POINT

23
28

Teacher Check _____

Initial   Date

My Score

page 43 (forty-three)

Before taking the LIFEPAC Test, you should do these self checks.

1. _____   Did you do good work on your last Self Test?

2. _____   Did you study again those parts of the LIFEPAC you didn't remember?

Check one: ☐ Yes (good)
            ☐ No (ask your teacher)

3. _____   Do you know all the new words in "Words to Study"?

Check one: ☐ Yes (good)
            ☐ No (ask your teacher)